Pickleball Parables

Inspiration On and Off the Court

Jackie Freeman

What People Are Saying
About Pickleball Parables

"Pickleball and faith—what a winning combination! In *Pickleball Parables,* author Jackie Freeman skillfully weaves together the joy of the game with deep spiritual truths, offering encouragement for both the court and life. Whether you're a passionate player or just starting out, this devotional will up lift your heart and strengthen your walk with Christ!"

—**Carol Kent,** Executive Director of Speak Up Ministries, speaker and author of *He Holds My Hand: Experiencing God's Presence and Protection*

"It is a rare gift when two passions—one to walk with Jesus Christ and one to walk on the court in pickleball—can come together in such a powerful way. In this devotional, my friend and fellow pickleball enthusiast, Jackie Freeman, invites us into a unique journey of growth, both on and off the pickleball court. With wisdom drawn from her own experiences, Jackie shares how this simple yet dynamic sport can teach us profound lessons about our walk with God. Pickleball, like life, is filled with moments of challenge, joy, failure, and victory. But through it all, we are reminded that God is with us in every serve, every volley, and every point. Just as we learn to rely on strategy, teamwork, and resilience in pickleball, we are also called to lean upon God's strength, trust His plan, and play with purpose in the adventurous game of life.

Jackie's heart for both the game and the gospel shines through every page of this devotional. She encourages us not only to sharpen our skills on the court but to deepen our faith and draw nearer to God through every encounter and every challenge. Whether you're a seasoned player or just beginning to pick up a paddle, this devotional will inspire you to live intentionally, loving God and others, both on the court and off. May you find encouragement in these pages, and may your faith grow stronger with each game, on every court, and in every moment of your journey. Thank you, Jackie, for the inspiration."

—**Jeff Sheeks**, Senior Pastor of First Baptist Church, Brooklyn, MI

"I am honored to recommend Jackie Freeman's devotional, *Pickleball Parables*! Her insightful, concise, and relevant daily devotions will challenge, educate, and uniquely uplift pickleball players. Like the quick reactions and agility required to play the sport well, Jackie has allowed God to weave her rich life experiences and deep faith into a playbook (game plan) for everyday living. Her devotions meet us all right where we are. Each parable improves our ability to bounce back no matter what is served our way.

As a health and fitness professional, I've truly appreciated Jackie's genuine drive to learn, grow, and master every skill that helps her be strong, agile, and flexible. Her positive, encouraging, and fun spirit gives her words a delightful approachability. And her enthusiastic willingness to dig in and truly learn this sport, as well as what God seeks to teach her through life's ups and downs, has given her the unique ability to bless, inspire, and encourage players of all ages and abilities. Just as you enjoy picking up your paddle and stepping out on that court for a lively, challenging game, pick up this book and embrace the fresh parallels Jackie draws between the sport she loves and the faith she lives. See how it deepens your own game, on and off the court!"

—**Laura Gurney**, Personal Trainer, ACE-CPT, Cancer Exercise Specialist (CES), Cancer Exercise Training Institute (CETI), The Centre, Adrian, MI

"This book is going to be a hit and is going to be one of a kind. *Pickleball Parables* shines a spotlight on the various facets of pickleball and illustrates how the game can mirror our everyday habits and foster a deeper appreciation for the countless blessings we encounter both on and off the court. It's an enjoyable, insightful, and lighthearted read that makes it easy for anyone to connect with its message."

—**Karen Worthy**, coauthor of the children's picture book *Bend Your Knees, Louise! A Pickleball Primer* and a pickleball enthusiast

"This is a must-read for anyone interested in the game of pickleball. Jackie is passionate about pickleball and deeply committed to her relationship with Christ. She beautifully illustrates how you can embrace both, showing how the sport of pickleball can draw you closer to God. As a midlife triathlete, I resonate with the idea that engaging in your sport can be a way to connect with God. Jackie not only teaches you how to do this but also guides you through the ins and outs of pickleball. What a refreshing and enjoyable read!"

—**Dr. Nancy Meyer**, Courage Coach, Speaker, and Author of *Defying Fear: Finding the Courage to Embrace Your True Value*

"*Pickleball Parables* brilliantly weaves together the joy of America's fastest-growing sport with profound spiritual insights. Even as someone who has never played pickleball, I found her analogies between court tactics and life's challenges remarkably thought-provoking. Jackie's warm, conversational style makes complex spiritual concepts accessible through the lens of pickleball, whether you're a seasoned player or just curious about the sport. Her personal stories of finding community and purpose after loss are especially touching, reminding us that God meets us exactly where we are—sometimes even on a pickleball court. This devotional is a perfect companion for anyone looking to deepen their faith journey, with or without a paddle in hand."

—**Christine Hoy**, Speaker and Author of *Peace Beyond Perfection*

Also by Jackie Freeman

Bend Your Knees, Louise!: A Pickleball Primer

Unwrapping Christmas:
Advent 4 Week Devotional

Keep a Song in Your Heart:
Musical Notes for Daily Devotions

A Journal for a JOYful Heart: songs of winter

A Journal for a JOYful Heart: songs of spring

A Journal for a JOYful Heart: songs of summer

A Journal for a JOYful Heart: songs of autumn

I'm Okay, Momma!

Strength in the Storm:
Real Stories. Real Women. Real Faith.

God with Us Immanuel
An Advent Devotional Through the Lineage of Christ

Print ISBN: 978-1-964511-08-5
eBook ISBN: 978-1-964511-09-2

To the One who orders my steps:

Thank You, God, for guiding me full circle from hesitant questions to unwavering faith. When I asked, "Where is faith in pickleball, Lord?" You patiently showed me that You are present in every aspect of life. This devotional is a testament to Your faithfulness, revealing that Your love and grace meet us wherever we go—on and off the court.

May each reader discover Your hand at work in their lives, one point at a time.

Game Plan

Strengthen Your Spiritual Game

Navigating Challenges

Reflecting God's Light

Final Reflection

A Note from Jackie

Pickleball Parables: Inspiration On and Off the Court blends a love for pickleball with a faith in God. Whether you're a seasoned player or just discovering this fun and fast-growing sport, this devotional is crafted to enrich your life both on and off the court.

Over the years, as I've grown as a player, I've found that time on the court often teaches lessons that stretch far beyond the game itself. If you, like me, seek inspiration through Scripture, personal stories, and practical applications, and if you love pickleball, I invite you to join me in a new and fun adventure. The principles we practice in pickleball—teamwork, perseverance, humility, and focus—parallel our spiritual journey.

Let's explore how pickleball can serve as a unique lens through which we deepen our love for the game and our faith in Christ.

This devotional is designed to be flexible, just like our game. Each reflection can stand alone, so you can move through them in order, jump to a topic that catches your eye, or use the book as a daily or weekly resource.

Here's one way to approach it:

Read and reflect on the Scripture that sets the foundation for each devotion. Then, let the story and its pickleball connection inspire and challenge you, on and off the court. End with the prayer as a starting point for a conversation with God.

So, grab your paddle, lace up your shoes, and stretch those muscles. Let's embark on this adventure together.

Jackie

"One thing I ask from the LORD,
this only do I seek: that I may dwell in the
hourse of the LORD all the days of my life,
to gaze on the beauty of the LORD
and to seek him in his temple."
Psalm 27:4 (NIV)

EMBRACING THE GAME

Ready Position:
Saying "Yes" to God's Call

Learning to trust God in the moment

"For God so loved the world, that he gave his only Son, that whoever believes in him should not perish but have eternal life." John 3:16 (ESV)

In pickleball, the ready position is everything. Knees slightly bent, paddle up, eyes focused—this stance prepares you to respond to whatever shot comes your way. Without it, you're caught off guard, scrambling to recover.

Life, much like pickleball, requires a ready position, a heart willing and prepared to say yes to God's call. Yet, stepping into something new can feel daunting. I know this firsthand.

After forty years of marriage, my husband's passing left me at a crossroads. The idea of stepping into new activities alone felt overwhelming.

But during farmhouse renovations, one of my carpenters casually suggested, "You should try pickleball. You'll like it." Skeptical but curious, I ventured into a gym where women of all ages were playing—and laughing. I wanted that kind of fun!

Pat Aben's warm welcome and the paddle she handed me marked the beginning of a new chapter in my life. What started as a simple invitation from acquaintances soon blossomed into deep friendships and a newfound love for a sport I never knew I needed. Looking back, I see how one yes led to open doors, a new community, and a fresh perspective on life.

Isn't that what faith is about? God calls us to step forward, even when we're unsure of what's ahead.

The greatest invitation we will ever receive is God's invitation to eternal life through Jesus. Just as I had to be willing to pick up a pickleball paddle and step onto the court, we must be willing to step out in faith and accept His love. Saying yes to Christ isn't about having it all figured out; it's about being in a ready position—open, willing, and prepared to follow Him.

Have you said yes to Jesus? His sacrifice on the cross is the ultimate expression of love. Through His death and resurrection, He offers salvation and the promise of eternal life. "For God so loved the world, that he gave his only Son, that whoever believes in him should not perish but have eternal life" (John 3:16).

Being in a ready position on the court prepares us for the next shot. Being in a ready position in faith prepares us for the life God has called us to live. Don't wait on the sidelines. Step forward and say yes today.

Dear Lord, thank You for loving me so much that You gave Your only Son to die on the cross and rise again for me. Help me stay in a ready position, always prepared to say yes to Your call. In Jesus' name, amen.

Your Game Plan

Take time to reflect and jot down your thoughts using these prompts:

IN PLAY: How can you put the principle from today's devotion into practice?

PADDLE UP: Write a prayer inspired by today's Scripture or message.

Warm Up for the Walk:
Preparing Your Mind and Heart

Getting ready for life's journey with Christ

"Train yourself for godliness; for while bodily training is of some value, godliness is of value in every way, as it holds promise for the present life and also for the life to come." 1 Timothy 4:7–8 (ESV)

I've walked onto the pickleball court without warming up more times than I care to admit. It usually starts with good intentions, jumping into the game enthusiastically, ready to give it my all. But as the game progresses, my stiff muscles remind me of my lack of preparation. If my partner happens to glance my way, I'm sure they're thinking, "She should've warmed up."

Physical readiness means more than warming up before and stretching after a game. It's about preparation, endurance, and recovery. Properly stretched muscles are more supple, less prone to injury, and ready to perform at their best. Skipping this step often results in slower starts, awkward movements, and regretful soreness later.

Our spiritual lives are much the same. If we fail to "warm up" daily by spending time with God through prayer, reading His Word, and inviting Him into our day, we can feel spiritually depleted, sluggish, and unprepared for the challenges ahead. Just as a game can reveal the consequences of skipping warm-ups, life shows us the importance of being spiritually prepared. In 1 Timothy 4:7–8, the apostle Paul encourages us to train ourselves for godliness, noting that while physical training has value, spiritual discipline benefits us both now and for eternity. Just as bending and stretching help us perform better physically, spending time with God prepares our hearts and minds to respond with grace, patience, and wisdom throughout the day.

"Cooling down" is as valuable as warming up. After a game or a long day, taking time to reflect, thank God, and seek His peace allows us to recover and grow. During these moments of stillness, we find renewed strength for the next challenge.

So, before you dive into your next game, or your next day, take time to warm up spiritually. Start the day with a prayer, meditate on a verse, and stretch your heart toward God. Your day will go smoother, and you'll find yourself better equipped to handle whatever comes your way.

Lord, thank You for reminding me that preparation is key in both physical and spiritual life. Help me start each day by warming up my heart with Your Word and seeking Your guidance. And may I end each day praising You for a day well lived. In Jesus' name, amen.

Your Game Plan

Take time to reflect and jot down your thoughts using these prompts:

IN PLAY: How can you put the principle from today's devotion into practice?

PADDLE UP: Write a prayer inspired by today's Scripture or message.

Pick Your Paddle:
Equipped for the Game of Life

Using the tools God gives us for His purpose

"Trust in the Lord with all your heart and lean not on your own understanding; in all your ways submit to him, and he will make your paths straight." Proverbs 3:5–6 (NIV)

When I first started playing pickleball, I was overwhelmed by the sheer number of paddle choices. Lightweight, heavyweight, thick grip, thin grip—who knew so many options existed? A friend once offered me his paddle to try, and I felt like I was wielding a sledgehammer. Every shot I made went rogue, as if the ball had a mind of its own, and that mind was saying, "Nope, not today!" I quickly learned that the wrong paddle makes the game unnecessarily difficult.

Choosing a paddle is a lot like deciding how to equip yourself for your spiritual walk. Just as our paddles should match our skill, strength, and playing style, God's Word is the basis for developing and applying godly principles in our daily walk.

Pickleball paddles have three key considerations: weight, grip size, and core material. Similarly, we need to weigh the importance of Scripture, grip the truth tightly, and let the core of God's Word guide our lives.

Weight: In pickleball, a heavier paddle provides power but can feel overwhelming if we're not ready for it. Trying to carry too much weight in life, such as other people's opinions and unnecessary worries, can leave us exhausted. God's Word reminds us to lean on His strength, not our own (Matthew 11:28–30).

Grip Size: A grip too large makes control difficult; too small, and we'll feel unstable. Spiritually, our grip on God's Word matters. A casual grip may leave us vulnerable, but a firm hold, rooted in trust and obedience, will keep us steady.

Core Material: Paddles are constructed from different materials for power and control. Similarly, our faith's "core material"—our heart and trust in God—determines our strength during trials. Proverbs 3:5–6 calls us to wholeheartedly trust Him, even when life's shots come at us fast.

God has provided the perfect "paddle" in His Word, equipping us to handle life's challenges with precision, power, and grace. Similarly, in pickleball, we react because we've prepared and practiced, creating muscle memory. When we memorize Scripture, the heart's memory muscle enables us to react as God's children.

Let's strengthen our grip this week by memorizing today's verse in Proverbs.

Lord, thank You for equipping us with everything we need through Your Word. Strengthen our grip on Your truth so we can navigate life's challenges with confidence and faith. In Jesus' name, amen.

Your Game Plan

Take time to reflect and jot down your thoughts using these prompts:

IN PLAY: How can you put the principle from today's devotion into practice?

PADDLE UP: Write a prayer inspired by today's Scripture or message.

Finding Your Court:
Where God Has Placed You

Serving Him right where you are

"Nevertheless, each person should live as a believer in whatever situation the Lord has assigned to them, just as God has called them."
1 Corinthians 7:17 (NIV)

When I began playing pickleball, I knew my place: watching, learning, and playing. Pickleball is one of those rare sports where seasoned players genuinely want to help newbies. I appreciated their patience and willingness to show me the ropes.

As a beginner, I spent a lot of time on Court 1, the entry-level court in our structured play format known as "King's Court." Here's how it works: advanced players start on Court 3, intermediate players on Court 2, and beginners on Court 1. After each game, the winners move up, while the losers move down.

Staying on Court 1 wasn't glamorous, but that was where I learned the rules, practiced my serves, and gained confidence in my abilities. Over time, the basics became second nature, and before I knew it, I started "moving up."

I'll never forget the day I landed on Court 3. My partner and I found ourselves facing an older gentleman who was well-known for his skills and competitive nature. I could tell he wasn't thrilled to see a "rookie" like me sharing his court. But as the game progressed, something remarkable happened: all those lessons from Court 1 paid off. My partner and I played well—so well, in fact, we won.

The look on our older opponent's face was priceless. He had to move down a court, and while I tried to suppress my grin, I couldn't help but feel proud. That day, I realized that every step of the journey had prepared me for where I was standing.

Isn't life a bit like finding your court?

God places us where we need to be, not necessarily where we want to be. Sometimes, we feel stuck on Court 1, wondering when we'll "level up." But it's on those lower courts, those places of learning, growth, and humility, where God prepares us for what is ahead.

As 1 Corinthians 7:17 reminds us, our court—our place—isn't an accident. God is using our current situation to equip us for His purpose. So, the next time we feel out of place or frustrated with our situation, let's remember that God has placed us on this court for a reason. We need to trust His timing, embrace the process, and play the game with faith and perseverance.

Lord, help us trust Your plan, even when we feel stuck or overlooked. Give us the patience to grow where we're planted, and may we always reflect Your love, no matter our circumstances. In Jesus' name, amen.

Your Game Plan

Take time to reflect and jot down your thoughts using these prompts:

IN PLAY: How can you put the principle from today's devotion into practice?

PADDLE UP: Write a prayer inspired by today's Scripture or message.

The First Serve:
Answering God's Call

Taking the first step of faith

"For anyone out there who doesn't know where you are going, anyone groping in the dark, here's what: Trust in God. Lean on your God."
Isaiah 50:10 (MSG)

In pickleball, the first serve is crucial. It sets the tone for the game, establishes control, and may eventually allow the players to claim victory. A successful serve opens the door for everything that follows. Similarly, answering God's call is like taking that first serve in our spiritual journey. It's our initial step in a lifelong game of faith, and just like pickleball, it can feel daunting, but it is essential.

Every time I stand on the court, paddle in hand, ready to open the game with my serve, I feel the weight of the moment. I know that if I miss that first serve, I forfeit the right to serve, and our opponents take over. I never want to let my partner down. They're counting on me to set the tone for the game. But at times, my serve has been a disaster, going wildly off target. In that moment, my partner's reassuring smile reminds me that we all miss sometimes, and the key is how we recover.

That serves as a reminder of life's bigger picture. As in pickleball, when we are called to something—whether by God or through our own life circumstances—it's easy to fear messing up. But the beauty of the first serve, in pickleball and our spiritual walk, is that perfection is not the goal. It's showing up, stepping up, and trusting God for the outcome.

In the past, I've hesitated when I felt God was calling me to something bigger than I was comfortable with. Maybe you've been there, too, hearing that gentle whisper to step out and serve in a new way. The question is this: Will we step forward in faith, even when we don't have it all figured out? In my experience, when I have taken that first step, God always meets me with His grace and guidance, much like a good partner does after a bad serve in pickleball.

God's call isn't about being perfect. It's about being willing. He needs us to answer the call, take the first step, and keep moving forward, serve after serve.

Have you ever felt God calling you to something new but hesitated to take that first step? What might happen if you trusted Him?

Lord, thank You for guiding us through each challenge that is served in our direction. May we serve and return what is served to us with courage, grace, and fortitude, knowing that You are with us in every game of life. In Jesus' name, amen.

Your Game Plan

Take time to reflect and jot down your thoughts using these prompts:

IN PLAY: How can you put the principle from today's devotion into practice?

PADDLE UP: Write a prayer inspired by today's Scripture or message.

The Dink Shot:
Small Actions, Big Impact

How small, consistent acts of faith change the world

"And whatever you do, in word or deed, do everything in the name of the Lord Jesus, giving thanks to God the Father through him."
Colossians 3:17 (ESV)

One essential skill for any pickleball player is mastering the dink shot, a soft, controlled shot that arcs over the net and lands in our opponents' non-volley zone (commonly called "the kitchen"). This move requires patience and precision. The goal is to land the ball near your opponents' net, making it difficult for them to return. Watching professional players execute this technique demonstrates how critical these shots are to their success. In fact, more games are won at the net with a well-placed dink shot than with any flashy smash.

When it comes to our faith journey, we often dream of the big wins—the grand gestures, life-changing moments, or monumental callings. But God frequently works through small, everyday actions. A kind word, a helping hand, or a prayer for someone in need may seem insignificant, but they ripple outward with eternal impact.

Ministry doesn't have to happen in big arenas or foreign mission fields. It happens when we faithfully love others, serve where we find ourselves, and walk in step with God's plan. In the little moments of obedience, we reflect His heart. Just like the dink shot requires focus and precision, living a life of small but meaningful actions requires intentionality and trust in God's purpose for each step we take.

Let's take time this week to perform small acts of kindness that reflect Christ's love. Consider writing a note or texting someone with an encouraging message or bringing a meal to someone in need. We need to remember that these small acts, done in faith and love, can significantly impact someone's life and God's kingdom.

Lord, thank You for reminding us that even the smallest acts of faith and kindness can make a significant impact. Teach us to be patient, purposeful, and faithful in the little things, trusting that You will use us for Your glory. May our actions, no matter how small, point others to You. In Jesus' name, amen.

Your Game Plan

Take time to reflect and jot down your thoughts using these prompts:

IN PLAY: How can you put the principle from today's devotion into practice?

PADDLE UP: Write a prayer inspired by today's Scripture or message.

GROWING IN FAITH

Perfect Your Serve:
Living with Purpose and Intention

Aligning your actions with God's will

"As each has received a gift, use it to serve one another, as good stewards of God's varied grace." 1 Peter 4:10 (ESV)

By now, it's no secret how wildly popular pickleball has become. Combining elements of tennis, badminton, and ping-pong, this sport has earned the title of the fastest-growing sport in America.

To start, mastering the serve is crucial. The underhand stroke is foundational, requiring the paddle to strike the ball below the waist. Even with the new option for a drop serve, the fundamental rule remains the same: We must make solid contact with the ball below our waist.

Aiming is half the battle. A seasoned player once suggested I consider placing a Hula-Hoop in the diagonal service box to practice accuracy. The concept was simple yet profound: "If you aim at nothing, you'll hit nothing every time."

In my early days, I developed a bad habit of rushing my serve. I thought speed equaled skill, but more often than not, I'd miss the shot and lose the serve. Thankfully, a wise mentor gently corrected me. "Slow down," he said. "Take a breath. You have the ball—take control and make them play your game."

Thanks to that advice, I developed a serving routine: Make eye contact with my opponent, announce the score, glance at my paddle, pause, and then serve. I chuckled when someone asked what I was doing when I looked at my paddle. Was I reading notes? Praying? Not quite, though prayer might have been a good idea!

Instead, I was remembering my mentor's advice to take my time and be intentional.

This lesson reminds me of Peter's words in 1 Peter 4:10, urging us to serve others as faithful stewards of God's grace. Just as in pickleball, serving isn't about waiting for perfect conditions or choosing whom we'd prefer to serve. We are called to serve whoever God places before us, even when anticipating a challenging "return."

We can be intentional in serving Him, even when we feel unprepared or inadequate. When we lean on His strength instead of our own, our weaknesses become opportunities for His power to shine. As Paul quoted the Lord in 2 Corinthians 12:9 (NLT), "My grace is all you need. My power works best in weakness."

Serving is more than an action. It reflects our devotion to Christ. Each act of service, no matter how small, is an opportunity to shine His light into the world.

Dear Lord, thank You for the privilege of serving You by serving others. Help us rely on Your strength so we may serve with Your grace. In Jesus' name, amen.

Your Game Plan

Take time to reflect and jot down your thoughts using these prompts:

IN PLAY: How can you put the principle from today's devotion into practice?

PADDLE UP: Write a prayer inspired by today's Scripture or message.

Keep Your Eye on the Ball: Staying Focused on What Matters

Keeping your faith central in life's chaos

"... fixing our eyes on Jesus, the pioneer and perfecter of faith. For the joy set before him he endured the cross, scorning its shame, and sat down at the right hand of the throne of God." Hebrews 12:2 (NIV)

For pickleball, as for many other sports, the best advice is "Keep your eye on the ball!" That's practically a mantra on the court, shouted by well-meaning partners, as if saying it louder will magically improve your game. They mean well, of course, but it's not always easy to focus when the ball darts like a firefly and your opponent's paddle looks ready to swat it into oblivion.

Life can feel the same—the ball flying back and forth between family, work, health, faith, and the never-ending to-do list. It's easy to lose focus, get distracted, and miss what matters most. The Bible, however, gives us clear guidance: Fix your eyes on Jesus.

In pickleball, we're bound to make mistakes when we take our eyes off the ball. We might swing too soon, too late, or miss entirely (and let's not even talk about that embarrassing whiff shot). Similarly, in life, when we take our eyes off Jesus, it's easy to stumble. We lose sight of His plan, His presence, and His purpose for our lives.

Hebrews 12:2 reminds us that Jesus endured the ultimate for us. He didn't waver, even under the weight of the cross. He kept His focus on the joy set before Him: our salvation and eternal life with Him. If He could remain steadfast in the face of overwhelming adversity, surely we can learn to stay focused on Him through our daily trials.

So, how do we keep our eyes on Jesus when life gets chaotic? We can start by spending time in His Word, praying, and surrounding ourselves with godly influences. It's about intentionally focusing on Him instead of the distractions and worries around us.

Remember, just like in pickleball, our focus determines the end results. In Philippians 3:13 (NLT), Paul writes, "I focus on this one thing: Forgetting the past and looking forward to what lies ahead."

Lord, thank You for being the steady focus in our fast-paced, sometimes confusing, ever-changing lives. Teach us to fix our eyes on You, no matter how chaotic things become. Help us trust Your plan, lean into Your presence, and find joy in the journey. In Jesus' name, amen.

Your Game Plan

Take time to reflect and jot down your thoughts using these prompts:

IN PLAY: How can you put the principle from today's devotion into practice?

PADDLE UP: Write a prayer inspired by today's Scripture or message.

Keep Moving Forward:
Turning Obstacles into Opportunities

Finding God's purpose in your struggles

"But one thing I do: Forgetting what is behind and straining toward
what is ahead, I press on toward the goal to win the prize for which
God has called me heavenward in Christ Jesus."
Philippians 3:13–14 (NIV)

Pickleball players dread the lob shot, the high, arching ball designed to fly just out of reach and force us into a difficult position. These shots can feel personal for someone like me, whose height does not lend itself to an overhead smash. Early on, I instinctively ran backward to try and reach them—a dangerous move that throws off our balance and often leads to injury. But over time, I've learned how to handle it: pivot, turn my body, and sprint toward the spot where the ball will land.

As you know, changing direction under this pressure is not easy. The temptation to backpedal is strong, both on the court and in life. How many times have we found ourselves looking backward, dwelling on mistakes, or lamenting what could have been? It's easy to replay past failures, thinking, "If only I had done this differently."

But God doesn't want us to live in reverse. The apostle Paul reminds us to forget what is behind and strain toward what is ahead. God has a purpose for our lives that requires us to pivot, adjust, and keep moving forward, no matter how many "lob shots" life throws at us.

There will be moments when we feel our challenges are too big and the setbacks too frequent. Like opponents who relentlessly target our weaknesses, life's struggles can feel overwhelming. In those moments, it's important to remember that God's strength is made perfect in our weaknesses (2 Corinthians 12:9).

When our prayers seem unanswered or when God feels silent, we should not run backward. We should pivot, change our perspective, seek God's guidance, and trust He is leading us toward something greater, even if we can't see it yet.

So, let's practice our pivot. Let's stop focusing on what's behind us (past mistakes and fears) and start anticipating where God is leading us next. And remember, the lob shot is not meant to defeat us. It's intended to test our focus and our faith. Let's take time to intentionally pivot by surrendering our struggles to God in prayer.

Lord, I confess that I often find myself looking back, holding onto past regrets. Help me let go of what lies behind me and press forward in life, following Your calling. In Jesus' name, amen.

Your Game Plan

Take time to reflect and jot down your thoughts using these prompts:

In Play: How can you put the principle from today's devotion into practice?

Paddle Up: Write a prayer inspired by today's Scripture or message.

Tethered Together:
Staying in Sync with God and Others

Building relationships rooted in Christ

"Since we live by the Spirit, let us keep in step with the Spirit."
Galatians 5:25 (NIV)

In pickleball, staying in tandem with your partner is essential for success. Imagine a six-foot rope tethering you to your partner. If our partners move left, we move left. If they step forward, we step forward. The idea is to cover the court as a team, seamlessly moving as one.

But what happens when our partners don't move with us? Maybe they linger at the baseline or hang out in the dreaded "no man's land," leaving us exposed. Trust me, I have been there and felt the frustration. You are ready to move forward to the kitchen line, but they're holding you back, disrupting the rhythm of the game.

I wonder how often God feels the same way about me. How often have I dashed ahead, expecting Him to follow instead of waiting on His timing? Or worse, how often have I lagged behind, hesitant to step into what He's calling me to do? Just like in pickleball, remaining tethered requires intentionality.

I need regular drills to strengthen my faith so I can move in step with God. A quick skim of Scripture or a half-hearted prayer won't cut it. Actual spiritual growth comes from dedicating time to studying the Bible, reflecting on His promises, and genuinely seeking His guidance. The more time I spend with Him, the more I learn His voice and His plan for me.

Like a well-synchronized pickleball partnership, being tethered to God brings peace and purpose, no matter what comes our way. Staying close to God following my husband's death helped me navigate through my grief. I understood what Hebrews 11:8 (NLT) meant: "It was by faith that Abraham obeyed when God called him to leave home and go to another land that God would give him as his inheritance. He went without knowing where he was going." Widowhood was the uncharted path for me.

Let's ask ourselves on a regular basis: Are we moving in tandem with God, or are we trying to pull Him in our direction?

Heavenly Father, thank You for guiding us even when we try to run ahead or hold back. Help us stay tethered to You, trusting Your timing and direction. Teach us to walk in step with Your Spirit, moving forward with purpose and faith. Thank You for Your grace when we fall short. In Jesus' name, amen.

Your Game Plan

Take time to reflect and jot down your thoughts using these prompts:

IN PLAY: How can you put the principle from today's devotion into practice?

PADDLE UP: Write a prayer inspired by today's Scripture or message.

No Sorries:
Living with Grace and Accountability

Choosing forgiveness over guilt

"Let your 'Yes' be 'Yes,' and your 'No,' 'No.' For whatever is more than these is from the evil one." Matthew 5:37 (NKJV)

When I first started playing pickleball, I said, "I'm sorry," more times than I care to count. A missed shot, a failed return, or even a poorly placed lob—out came the apology. One day, my friends decided enough was enough. They declared, "There are no sorries in pickleball!" They introduced a fine to ensure I got the message. Every time I said, "I'm sorry," I owed them $1. Let me say that they ate well that night at my expense!

Looking back, I realize those constant apologies weren't just about the game; they reflected a deeper struggle to accept my imperfections and let go of unnecessary guilt. How often do we say "I'm sorry" out of habit or because we feel obligated, not because we genuinely mean it?

In life, as in pickleball, our words matter. Jesus taught us to let our words be simple, honest, and meaningful: "Let your 'Yes' be 'Yes,' and your 'No,' 'No'" (Matthew 5:37). This includes apologies. Saying "I'm sorry" should be more than a reflex; it should come from a sincere heart when we've truly wronged someone.

But what about those times when we feel compelled to apologize for things beyond our control? Maybe it's a fear of disappointing others or an attempt to smooth over awkward moments. The truth is that not everything requires an apology. Sometimes, we need to give ourselves grace.

Instead of over-apologizing, let's focus on living with integrity and grace. When we need to say, "I'm sorry," let it be a heartfelt acknowledgment of wrongdoing coupled with a commitment to make things right. Let's trust that God's grace covers our imperfections, freeing us to live confidently in His love.

So, the next time you feel an unnecessary "I'm sorry" creeping up, pause and smile. Remember the lesson from my pickleball friends and save yourself the dinner bill. Let your words reflect a heart that's sincere, confident, and grounded in God's grace. But let us also remember to offer a heartfelt apology when necessary—and may God give us the wisdom to know the difference.

Lord, thank You for teaching us the power of our words. Please help us to speak with honesty and sincerity. Remind us that Your love covers our imperfections, and we don't have to carry unnecessary guilt. In Jesus' name, amen.

Your Game Plan

Take time to reflect and jot down your thoughts using these prompts:

IN PLAY: How can you put the principle from today's devotion into practice?

PADDLE UP: Write a prayer inspired by today's Scripture or message.

A Rulebook That Never Changes: Grounded in God's Word

Finding stability and truth in the Bible

"For the word of God is alive and active. Sharper than any double-edged sword, it penetrates even to dividing soul and spirit, joints and marrow; it judges the thoughts and attitudes of the heart."
Hebrews 4:12 (NIV)

Pickleball enthusiasts know the excitement, and occasional frustration, that comes with the annual rule changes from the USA Pickleball Association. Every year, new suggestions are submitted, reviewed, and sometimes added to the official rulebook. Some changes make sense, while others leave us scratching our heads. I'm grateful that most rules remain the same, giving structure to the game I love.

This process reminds me of something far more significant: the Word of God. Unlike pickleball rules, the Bible doesn't change with the times or adapt to cultural trends. God's Word is eternal and unshakeable. Psalm 119:89 (NIV) declares, "Your word, Lord, is eternal; it stands firm in the heavens."

However, in today's world, many people rely on secondhand Scripture information. They listen to podcasts, follow inspirational social media accounts, or take a friend's word for what the Bible says. While those resources can be helpful, they're no substitute for digging into God's Word. Imagine playing a game of pickleball based solely on someone else's opinion of the rules. Most of us have played pickleball with someone who thinks they know it all, right?

As Christians, we need to know the" rulebook" for ourselves. The Bible is not just a collection of suggestions or ancient guidelines; it's a living, active roadmap for our faith. Hebrews 4:12 describes it as a double-edged sword, judging the thoughts and attitudes of the heart.

Unlike the yearly updates to the pickleball rulebook, God's Word is flawless and complete. We don't have to wait for committee reviews or board of director approvals to know what's true. It's all there, unchanging, from Genesis to Revelation.

So, let's commit to being students of the Word. Let's open our Bibles daily, meditate on God's truths, and apply His teachings to our lives. Remember, we read the Bible for information, transformation, and inspiration. We don't have to rely on secondhand interpretations or wait for updates. God's truth is already perfect, timeless, and sufficient.

Heavenly Father, thank You for giving us Your unchanging Word to guide our lives. Help us treasure it, read it, and live by it daily. In Jesus' name, amen.

Your Game Plan

Take time to reflect and jot down your thoughts using these prompts:

IN PLAY: How can you put the principle from today's devotion into practice?

PADDLE UP: Write a prayer inspired by today's Scripture or message.

STRENGTHEN YOUR SPIRITUAL GAME

Stay Out of the Kitchen:
Letting God Take the Lead

Trusting Him to guide your steps

"Those who know your name trust in you, for you, Lord, have never forsaken those who seek you." Psalm 9:10 (NIV)

In pickleball, the "kitchen" is a no-go zone—a seven-foot space on either side of the net where players can't volley the ball until after the first bounce. The purpose of the kitchen is to keep the game fair, to prevent players from dominating the net, and, let's be honest, to save us from overzealous kitchen dives. Yet how often do we ignore life's "kitchen rules" and dive into situations that aren't ours to handle?

I've been guilty of this. For years, I operated as little Miss Independent, taking on every problem that came my way. I thought it was my responsibility to fix everything: relationships, schedules, and even other people's messes. If life were a pickleball match, I was constantly rushing into the kitchen, thinking every shot was mine to take.

But here's the thing: That's not how God designed us to live. Like pickleball's kitchen rule helps maintain balance, God provides boundaries for us too. We're called to trust Him and step back, resisting the urge to fix, solve, and control, all of which can be challenging.

Exodus 14:14 (NIV) reminds us, "The Lord will fight for you; you need only to be still." This doesn't mean we sit on the sidelines and do nothing, but it does mean recognizing when a situation is better left in God's hands. Sometimes, the best action we can take is to pray, wait, and let God work in ways only He can.

Much like learning to honor pickleball's kitchen rule, stepping back in life takes practice and humility. It's not easy to resist the pull to jump in, especially when we're wired to think independence is strength. True strength is found in dependence on God.

This week, let's identify an area where we've been stepping into the "kitchen," trying to take control. Let's commit to stepping back and trusting God to handle it. When my impulse is to sweep in, I need to ask myself a clarifying question: "Is this mine to do, or am I called to wait on God?"

Lord, thank You for holding everything together. Forgive us for the times we've rushed in, thinking it was our job to fix what only You can handle. Help us honor Your boundaries and find peace in Your plan. In Jesus' name, amen.

Your Game Plan

Take time to reflect and jot down your thoughts using these prompts:

IN PLAY: How can you put the principle from today's devotion into practice?

PADDLE UP: Write a prayer inspired by today's Scripture or message.

Spiritual and Physical Hydration: Nourishing Soul and Body

Prioritizing spiritual health alongside physical well-being

"But whoever drinks of the water that I will give him will never be thirsty again. The water that I will give him will become in him a spring of water welling up to eternal life." John 4:14 (ESV)

Staying hydrated is vital for our well-being. Our bodies rely on water to function properly; we cannot survive without water. We've all seen athletes falter due to dehydration. The sudden drop in energy can be avoided with water breaks. Experts recommend drinking about half our body weight in ounces of water daily to keep our bodies running at our best.

Staying hydrated is crucial whether we're playing pickleball or simply going about our day. Yet, this got me thinking: What about our *spiritual hydration*?

How often do we neglect our spiritual nourishment—praying, studying Scripture, or spending time in God's presence—only to find ourselves spiritually parched? Are there areas in your life where you feel spiritually dehydrated? I know I've had some!

In John 4, Jesus has a powerful encounter with a Samaritan woman at a well. He speaks to her about water that goes beyond physical thirst, offering her something eternal. "But whoever drinks of the water that I will give him will never be thirsty again. The water that I will give him will become in him a spring of water welling up to eternal life" (John 4:14 ESV).

This conversation reminds me that the living water Jesus offers satisfies our deepest spiritual thirst. It's also a beautiful example of how salvation is for everyone, no matter our past or where we come from.

And unlike water, which has specific daily recommendations, there's no limit to how much time we can spend in fellowship with God or studying His Word. How will you spiritually rehydrate yourself and drink from the well that never runs dry today? I encourage you to read and meditate on God's Word or simply sit in His presence.

Dear Lord, thank You for offering living water that satisfies our souls. Help us to crave Your presence and prioritize time with You daily. May Your Word refresh us and flow through us, bringing light and love to others. In Jesus' name, amen.

Your Game Plan

Take time to reflect and jot down your thoughts using these prompts:

IN PLAY: How can you put the principle from today's devotion into practice?

PADDLE UP: Write a prayer inspired by today's Scripture or message.

Anticipation:
Staying Spiritually Alert

Being ready for God's opportunities

"Be alert and of sober mind. Your enemy the devil prowls around like a roaring lion looking for someone to devour." 1 Peter 5:8 (NIV)

As someone who graduated before Title IX, I didn't grow up learning sports strategy. Sideline cheer and band were the only options available to girls in my generation. So, when I started playing pickleball, I had to learn the basics from the ground up. In my early days, I focused solely on developing my skills because that was all I could handle.

As I improved, I realized the game required more than just my own abilities. I learned to progress from reacting to anticipating my opponents' next move. I learned to watch their swing, paddle position, and body language to prepare myself for where the ball might go next. I learned that their eyes usually reveal where the ball is headed.

But I've been caught off guard more times than I'd like to admit. I've stood frozen in the middle of a rally, suddenly realizing the ball was coming straight for me. It's a moment of panic, a deer-in-the-headlights feeling. These experiences taught me to stay ready, always expecting that the next shot could come my way.

This lesson on the pickleball court reminds me of our spiritual lives. Just when we think we've got life figured out, Satan shows up, ready to throw us off balance. Scripture warns us in I Peter 5:8, "Be alert and of sober mind. Your enemy the devil prowls around like a roaring lion looking for someone to devour."

Satan's attacks are as inevitable as the next shot on the court. He seeks to disrupt our focus, our faith, and our confidence. His approach isn't always enticing us with bad things. He will even use something good to keep us from devoting our best to God. No matter how much we know the Bible or how active we are in prayer, we must be spiritually vigilant.

So, how do we prepare? By staying connected to God through memorizing His Word, prayer, and the support of fellow believers. As we watch our opponent's moves on the court, we need to watch out for the ways Satan tries to distract or deceive us. And when his "ball" comes our way, we can stand firm, ready to respond with the truth of God's promises.

This week, let's examine where we might be spiritually unprepared or distracted. I'm going to ask God to help me stay alert and ready to face any challenges with His strength and guidance. What about you?

Lord, thank You for the reminder to stay alert and watchful in our walk with You. Teach us to anticipate the enemy's attacks and respond with Your truth and grace. In Jesus' name, amen.

Your Game Plan

Take time to reflect and jot down your thoughts using these prompts:

IN PLAY: How can you put the principle from today's devotion into practice?

PADDLE UP: Write a prayer inspired by today's Scripture or message.

The Sweet Spot:
Finding Joy in Our Walk with Christ

Discovering fulfillment in faith

"You make known to me the path of life; in your presence there is fullness of joy; at your right hand are pleasures forevermore." Psalm 16:11 (ESV)

In pickleball, the sweet spot is where the magic happens. Everything clicks when the ball makes contact with the center of the paddle. The shot is crisp, controlled, and powerful. But if we hit the ball too far on the edge, we'll end up with a wobbly mess of a return that might land somewhere near Mars—or in your opponent's slam zone.

The sweet spot doesn't happen by accident. It takes practice to find it consistently, to feel the rhythm and connection that allows you to strike with accuracy. Similarly, in our walk with Christ, joy is our sweet spot. It's not something we stumble upon by chance but something we cultivate by centering ourselves in Him.

Just as I can't find the sweet spot on my paddle without focus, I can't experience the fullness of joy without being intentional about seeking God's presence. When I rely on my own strength or get distracted by life's noisy sidelines, my spiritual "shots" feel off-balance. I can swing with all my might, but the result is weak and unfulfilling.

However, when I align my life with God and His perfect plan for my life, everything suddenly feels right. Even when life isn't ideal, I can rest in the joy that comes from knowing Him. Joy, after all, isn't just a fleeting feeling but a steady confidence that God is in control, no matter how intense the match of life gets. Nehemiah 8:10 (NIV) reminds us, "The joy of the Lord is your strength."

Have you been missing the sweet spot in your faith walk? Maybe it's time to refocus and find joy where it truly resides: in His presence. Let's take time today to center ourselves in Christ, allowing His joy to flow through us and give us the power to navigate life's challenges with grace.

Lord, thank You for being the source of our joy. Help us center our lives on You, focus on Your presence, and trust in Your strength. Make our lives reflect the joy and power that comes from walking closely with You without worldly distractions. In Jesus' name, amen.

Your Game Plan

Take time to reflect and jot down your thoughts using these prompts:

IN PLAY: How can you put the principle from today's devotion into practice?

PADDLE UP: Write a prayer inspired by today's Scripture or message.

Endurance in the Rally:
Pressing On When Life Gets Tough

Persevering with strength from God

"Blessed is the one who perseveres under trial because, having stood the test, that person will receive the crown of life that the Lord has promised to those who love him." James 1:12 (NIV)

Have you ever been in a pickleball rally that felt like it might last forever? Back and forth, the ball zips over the net while you scurry side to side like a squirrel in traffic, heart pounding, legs burning, wondering who will blink first. Then, just as you're about to break the rally with the perfect shot ... you hit the net. *Sigh.*

Pickleball rallies can be exhausting, but they teach us an important lesson: Endurance is the name of the game. We can't stop halfway through a rally and catch our breath. We press on, trusting our training and skills to carry us through. Life's challenges often feel like that endless rally. Whether it's a difficult season at work, a family struggle, or a health issue, we all face trials that test our perseverance.

In those moments, focusing on our weakness is tempting: our aching muscles, tired hearts, or weary minds. But just as pickleball players must keep their eyes on the ball, we are called to fix our eyes on God. He is our strength when we're weak and our guide when we're uncertain.

The Bible reminds us in James 1:12 that perseverance has its rewards. Hebrews 12:1–2 (NIV) echoes that thought: "Therefore, since we are surrounded by such a great cloud of witnesses, let us throw off everything that hinders and the sin that so easily entangles. And let us run with perseverance the race marked out for us, fixing our eyes on Jesus, the pioneer and perfecter of faith."

And let's not forget to laugh along the journey. A missed shot or two in pickleball isn't the end of the world (though it might feel like it in the moment). Life's setbacks are opportunities to trust God's timing and purpose. Perseverance isn't about perfection. It is about faithfulness.

So, the next time we're in a rally—on the court or in life—let's dig deep, keep swinging, and remember we're never playing alone. God's got our backs, and the eternal crown of life is worth every moment of effort.

Heavenly Father, thank You for walking with us through life's rallies. When the challenges seem unending, and our strength falters, remind us to trust in You. Help us persevere with faith and focus, knowing that Your plan is greater than any struggle we face. In Jesus' name, amen.

Your Game Plan

Take time to reflect and jot down your thoughts using these prompts:

IN PLAY: How can you put the principle from today's devotion into practice?

PADDLE UP: Write a prayer inspired by today's Scripture or message.

The Winning Shot:
Living for Eternal Rewards

Focusing on what truly matters

"Do not store up for yourselves treasures on earth, where moths and vermin destroy, and where thieves break in and steal. But store up for yourselves treasures in heaven." Matthew 6:19–20 (NIV)

Winning feels good, doesn't it? Whether snagging that gold medal in pickleball or acing a challenge at work, a victory is thrilling. But as shiny as medals and trophies can be, they're just temporary.

Sometimes, though, my competitive streak can get the best of me. I've found myself wanting to win not just for the fun of the game but for the glory of recognition. *Ouch.* It's humbling to realize how often my pride sneaks in, whispering, "Make sure everyone notices." And that humbling realization makes me ask myself: How often do I approach my spiritual walk with the same mindset?

Do I serve God for His glory or my own? Am I leading others to Christ with pure intentions, or am I keeping a secret scorecard, hoping to impress others with my "winning" faith? *Oof*, talk about a get-behind-me-Satan moment.

Jesus reminds us that life isn't about earthly accolades. The rewards that matter aren't gold medals or public recognition but the eternal treasures we store up in heaven. Our most significant and most coveted reward is our relationship with Jesus Christ, here and now. And it's just a taste of what's ahead.

So, as in pickleball, life's winning shot doesn't come from focusing on the scoreboard but from playing with purpose and joy. Our winning shot isn't about how many people notice our good deeds or how perfect our lives look. It comes from living a life that honors Jesus Christ, pointing others to Him through our actions and words.

The ultimate reward is hearing Him say, "Well done, good and faithful servant!" (Matthew 25:21 NIV). That's the kind of gold medal we should all strive for—not the applause of others but the approval of our Heavenly Father.

Lord, thank You for the reminder that life's true rewards are not found in this world but in eternity with You. Help us strive for Your approval, not the world's, to glorify You rather than ourselves. May our lives point others to You in everything we do and say. In Jesus' name, amen.

Your Game Plan

Take time to reflect and jot down your thoughts using these prompts:

In Play: How can you put the principle from today's devotion into practice?

Paddle Up: Write a prayer inspired by today's Scripture or message.

NAVIGATING CHALLENGES

Calling the Shots:
Staying Inside God's Lines

Living within His boundaries with purpose

"Whether you turn to the right or to the left, your ears will hear a
voice behind you, saying 'This is the way; walk in it.'"
Isaiah 31:21 (NIV)

As in life, pickleball is best played when the players understand the boundaries: 20 feet by 44 feet, to be exact. If you're lucky enough to have a proper playing area, it's recommended to make it 34 feet by 64 feet, with extra room for spectators. And, if you want to level up, position the court north to south to avoid squinting directly into the sun. Losing sight of a ball because it's directly in line with the sun is no fun.

Then there are those lines themselves: immovable and still debated. For example, if the serve lands on the kitchen line, it's a fault. Calling a ball "out of bounds" relies on the integrity of the receiving team. That rule has been known to ignite a few disagreements, but pickleball's golden rule is to *have fun*, so we try to move on quickly.

The lines on the court serve as a guide, just as God's Word guides our lives. We don't get to pick the court or move the lines to suit our game in pickleball. Similarly, in life, we don't always get to choose the court where God places us. Sometimes, it feels cramped; sometimes, the sun blinds us, and sometimes, the calls don't go in our favor. Yet, we are still called to serve and to serve faithfully.

Discernment is our spiritual line judge. Knowing when to speak, act, or step back requires wisdom only God can provide. Just as players rely on the court's boundaries, we rely on God's boundaries to make decisions that honor Him. His Word offers clarity when life feels murky, much like those crisp white lines on a pickleball court.

Here's the best part: When we rely on God's discernment, we can let go of the fear of making the wrong call. He promises to guide us, whether serving, receiving, or simply waiting for the next play.

Is there an area of your life where you need discernment right now? God's Word tells us He will give us wisdom when we ask for it. He does not withhold discernment. It's a benefit for believers, but we must seek it, ask for it, and take the time to receive it.

Lord, thank You for the boundaries and guidance You provide in our lives. Help us to trust You and serve You faithfully, even when the court feels challenging, or the calls seem unfair. May our lives always reflect Your wisdom and bring You glory. In Jesus' name, amen.

Your Game Plan

Take time to reflect and jot down your thoughts using these prompts:

IN PLAY: How can you put the principle from today's devotion into practice?

PADDLE UP: Write a prayer inspired by today's Scripture or message.

Grace for the Shots We Miss: Embracing Forgiveness

Learning to rely on God's grace

"My grace is sufficient for you, for my power is made perfect in weakness." 2 Corinthians 12:9 (NIV)

If there is one universal truth in pickleball, it's this: You're going to miss a shot. Maybe you didn't react fast enough, your aim was off, or you swung so hard that the ball practically landed in the next zip code. It happens to the best players.

In those moments, we're tempted to dwell on the missed shot. We replay it in our minds, wondering how we could have done better. Meanwhile, the game continues, and if we're not careful, we'll miss the next opportunity to make a great play.

Life is a lot like that. We all have moments we wish we could redo—words we shouldn't have said, decisions we regret, opportunities we missed. And yet, the beautiful truth of the gospel is this: God's grace covers all those regrettable moments.

Pickleball teaches us to keep moving forward. Sure, we missed the shot. But the match isn't over. There's another serve, another volley, another chance to play our best. In life, God offers the same hope. His grace is sufficient, even when we fumble. He rewards us for showing up, trying again, and trusting Him to guide us.

When we focus too much on our mistakes, we risk losing sight of what God is doing through us and in us. Instead of dwelling on where we fall short, let's celebrate the times we got it right—the acts of kindness we extended, the moments of courage we embraced, or the times we leaned on God when we could have given up.

The great thing about grace is that it is not earned. Grace is a gift of forgiveness and unmerited favor, freely given by a loving God who knows our weaknesses and loves us anyway. And if God can forgive us, shouldn't we forgive ourselves too?

So, the next time we miss a shot, on the court or in life, let's take a deep breath. Let it go. Focus on the next opportunity to do better. Because in the grand scheme of things, the missed points don't define us. What does define us is how we rise again, covered in grace and ready to keep playing.

Heavenly Father, thank You for Your grace that covers all our mistakes. Please help us to let go of the regrets and the times we've fallen short, and help us focus on opportunities You give us each day to serve You. Teach us to forgive ourselves and others as You have forgiven us. In Jesus' name, amen.

Your Game Plan

Take time to reflect and jot down your thoughts using these prompts:

In Play: How can you put the principle from today's devotion into practice?

Paddle Up: Write a prayer inspired by today's Scripture or message.

Life's Round-Robins:
Growing Through Every Match

Finding lessons in life's cycles

"As iron sharpens iron, so one person sharpens another."
Proverbs 27:17 (NIV)

In pickleball, the round-robin format guarantees that players face multiple opponents, testing their skills in various ways. While this can be time-consuming, it's also one of the best ways to improve as a player. Each match provides an opportunity to learn and grow.

Our spiritual journey mirrors this format. Life presents us with "matches" through interactions with family, friends, colleagues, and strangers. Every encounter is a divinely orchestrated opportunity for growth.

A Time to Refine

God uses our interactions to shape our character. Some matches are joyful and easy, like an uplifting conversation with a friend. Others are challenging, like an unexpected conflict or a difficult person. Each one refines us, as Proverbs 27:17 reminds us. Through our relationships, we sharpen our skills and grow compassion for one another.

A Time to Commit

Just as pickleball players must commit to their matches, we must be intentional in our spiritual lives. Practicing Christ-like love requires dedication. This discipline prepares us for the matches life throws our way.

A Time to Celebrate Growth

In a round-robin, every match contributes to players' scores, whether they win or lose. Similarly, every experience in life, whether good or bad, can lead to spiritual growth. We need to celebrate the moments we show up, give our best, and trust God to use them for His glory.

Life's round-robin isn't about a single defining moment but a series of encounters that, when viewed together, reveal God's hand at work. When I reflect on my recent matches, I need to ask myself, "How has God used them to sharpen my character?" I'm committing to approaching each day as an opportunity for spiritual growth, no matter the challenge. You are more than welcome to join me in this!

Lord, thank You for the "matches" You have placed in our lives. When we face challenges, remind us that You are using them to refine our character. Thank you for coaching us through life's round-robin. In Jesus' name, amen.

Your Game Plan

Take time to reflect and jot down your thoughts using these prompts:

IN PLAY: How can you put the principle from today's devotion into practice?

PADDLE UP: Write a prayer inspired by today's Scripture or message.

Game On:
Staying Focused in Faith and Pickleball

Keeping your priorities aligned with Christ

"We destroy arguments and every lofty opinion raised against the knowledge of God and take every thought captive to obey Christ."
2 Corinthians 10:5 (ESV)

Surprisingly, pickleball challenges my mind even more than my body. Between the rules, scoring, and sizing up opponents, I can easily get distracted. Add in a wandering mind that loves to review the day's to-do list or ponder tonight's dinner menu, and I have a recipe for disaster. Sound familiar?

My lack of focus cost my partner dearly during a recent round-robin pickleball tournament. Here's how it works: Partners rotate each match to keep things fair, and the final results depend on games won or points scored. There is no stacking the deck; it's just honest play. Fair enough, right?

But there I was, standing on the court, trying to juggle opponents, strategy, and (apparently) my attention span. Among the spectators, I spotted a friend having what looked like a serious conversation. My social butterfly instincts kicked in. I noticed her becoming distressed, crying, and walking away from the bleachers. Suddenly, my head wasn't in the game. I was consumed by worry, trying to guess what had upset her.

Naturally, my playing took a nosedive. While my partner valiantly kept us afloat, I missed each shot and gave away points, all because I wasn't fully present. The truth hit me: I'd failed my partner and myself by letting my focus drift away from the task at hand.

In life, we often do the same. We misdirect our attention, rushing to fix others' problems while neglecting our own priorities. It's noble to care for others, but not at the expense of what God and, often, our partners entrusted us to do.

As Paul reminds us in 2 Corinthians 10:5 (ESV), taking our thoughts captive means focusing on what's most important—God's calling for each of us at each moment.

So, what's the lesson? Keep our heads in the game. Whether it's pickleball or life, staying focused allows us to give our best and honor the role God has given us. The next time our attention wavers, let's ask God for the clarity and discipline to stay on course.

And yes, I checked on my friend after the tournament. It turns out she was fine. I witnessed a minor misunderstanding. But the real win that day was the reminder to play life's game with intentionality, trusting God to help me stay present where it matters most.

Heavenly Father, help us stop our wandering thoughts and focus on You, on and off the court. We need You every moment of the day, guiding us as we try to follow the path and plans You have for us. In Jesus' name, amen.

Your Game Plan

Take time to reflect and jot down your thoughts using these prompts:

In Play: How can you put the principle from today's devotion into practice?

Paddle Up: Write a prayer inspired by today's Scripture or message.

The Power of the Follow-Through: Faithfully Finishing Strong

Trusting God to complete His work in you

"Let us not grow weary of doing good, for in due season we will reap, if we do not give up." Galatians 6:9 (ESV)

In pickleball, success results from the follow-through. That means the shot doesn't end when we make contact with the ball. What comes after is critical. A solid follow-through ensures that our shots have the power, direction, and consistency needed to stay in play. If we stop our swing too soon, our shot will fall short, sometimes literally.

The same principle applies to our faith journey. Following through means committing fully to what God has called us to do, not just starting strong and fizzling out. We are called to persevere through the challenges, stay engaged, and see situations through to completion.

Think about Jesus' ministry. He didn't stop halfway through His mission. He followed through all the way to the cross and beyond. His commitment wasn't partial but complete, demonstrating that true love and obedience require follow-through.

But let's be honest: Following through in life can be challenging. It's easy to start strong when the excitement is high, but as the challenges come and the initial enthusiasm wanes, we might be tempted to stop short. Whether it's a new ministry, a tough conversation, or a commitment to prayer, the follow-through is what matters as we test our faith and endurance.

In pickleball, a strong follow-through often involves engaging our whole body—arms, legs, and core. In our faith, follow-through requires engaging our whole being—our heart, mind, soul, and strength. It requires us to stay connected to God through prayer, rely on His Word, and surround ourselves with a community that encourages us to press on.

Sometimes, we won't see the results of our efforts. A well-executed shot might win us a point immediately, but in faith, the reward is often seen later, in lives touched, seeds planted, and the character shaped. Galatians 6:9 reminds us not to grow weary in doing good, for the harvest will come if we persevere.

So, the next time you're on the court and hear someone remind you to "follow through," follow their advice, and afterward, consider how you can apply that to your walk with God.

Lord, thank You for being the ultimate example of follow-through. Help us to stay committed to the work You've called us to, even when it feels difficult or unfruitful. Teach is to rely on Your strength and not our own. May our lives reflect Your love and faithfulness as we pursue the critically important game of life. In Jesus' name, amen.

Your Game Plan

Take time to reflect and jot down your thoughts using these prompts:

IN PLAY: How can you put the principle from today's devotion into practice?

PADDLE UP: Write a prayer inspired by today's Scripture or message.

Playing the Part or Living the Faith: Walking in Authenticity

Choosing genuine faith over appearance

"These people honor me with their lips, but their hearts are far from me." Matthew 15:8 (NIV)

Shouldn't advertisers at least *try* to depict pickleball accurately in commercials if they intend to use it to sell something? I become downright frustrated when I see people pretending to play pickleball when they clearly don't have a clue.

Let me set the scene: A friend texted me, saying, "You've got to watch this!" Apparently, a popular TV show featuring an older bachelor (I'll let you guess the show) was introducing his potential partners to pickleball. Now, I wasn't sure if my friend wanted me to check out the show for the drama or the pickleball, but curiosity won out.

Big mistake.

There they were, flailing their paddles like they were trying to swat flies. Balls were flying in all directions. One lady was twirling her paddle like a baton in a parade. Strategy? Nonexistent. Strokes? Atrocious. Stances? All wrong. Clearly, no one had done any homework on how pickleball is played.

Were they having fun? Were they entertaining? Absolutely. But were they playing pickleball? Not even close.

As I grabbed the remote and changed the channel (before my blood pressure spiked), the show got me thinking: Is this how people see us as followers of Christ? Do we reflect God's truth, or are we just swinging paddles in all the wrong directions, hoping to look the part?

Those women weren't interested in learning real pickleball. They just wanted to look good and grab attention. But that's not what pickleball—or faith—is about.

Jesus encountered people like this all the time. The religious leaders of His day had their paddles all wrong too. They thought they were nailing it with their rules and rituals, but their hearts were far from God. Jesus reminded them and us that He came not for appearances but to seek and save the lost (Luke 19:10).

As believers, we can't just fake our faith. Faith requires intention, study, and a whole lot of grace. The Bible isn't just a rulebook; it's our playbook for life. If we don't spend time in it, we might find ourselves playing the game all wrong, just like those misguided "pickleballers" on TV.

Let's spend time in God's Word and ask Him to help us live authentically, not as if we're posturing for a television show or commercial. Unlike that TV show, life isn't about how we look on camera. It's about who we are when no one's watching.

Heavenly Father, help us honor You in everything we say and do. May our every action, reaction, thought, word, and deed be authentic and pleasing to You. In Jesus' name, amen.

Your Game Plan

Take time to reflect and jot down your thoughts using these prompts:

IN PLAY: How can you put the principle from today's devotion into practice?

PADDLE UP: Write a prayer inspired by today's Scripture or message.

REFLECTING GOD'S LIGHT

There's an App for That: Accessing God's Guidance

Turning to Him for direction in every season

"Do not merely listen to the word, and so deceive yourselves. Do what it says." James 1:22 (NIV)

In today's world, there's an app for practically everything, and the sport of pickleball is no exception. Need to find a court? Places2Play has you covered. Want to sharpen your skills with a virtual coach? Level-UP Fitness to the rescue! And if you're juggling multiple pickleball groups, apps such as TeamReach and GroupMe update you on local schedules and all the pickleball gossip.

I love staying connected, but with four pickleball groups buzzing on my phone, the notifications can get overwhelming. Sure, I've silenced them now and then (for my sanity), but I must admit, I appreciate those "ping" reminders for upcoming games. Even when I can't make it to the courts, those little nudges remind me to get moving or squeeze in some physical activity.

Pickleball isn't the only area where notifications play a role in my life. Bible apps, such as YouVersion, also send reminders—a verse of the day or a devotional to dive into. Yet, how often have I thought, "I'll read that later"? Too many times to count.

Here's the thing: Reminders, whether they're about pickleball or Scripture, are meaningless unless we take action. The apps can ping us all day long, but the choice to respond is ours. Will we dive into God's Word or prioritize other activities? Will we let the day's busyness crowd out our time for Him?

Think about it: If I only watched pickleball drills online but never practiced, my game wouldn't improve. The same principle applies to our spiritual growth. Listening to a sermon, reading a verse, or hearing a reminder is a great start, but God also calls us to action. As James 1:22 reminds us, we shouldn't just listen to the Word. We must do what it says.

Good intentions only take us so far. Without action, those intentions gather dust, and we're left with regret for what we didn't follow through on. Like improving a pickleball serve, spiritual growth doesn't happen by accident. It takes commitment, discipline, and, yes, showing up.

Don't hit snooze the next time you get a ping from your Bible app or feel a nudge to open God's Word. Treat it as an invitation to connect with your Creator. He is the ultimate coach, and His Word is the best training manual we could ever have.

Heavenly Father, alert us to Your call. We want to hear Your will and do Your will. Keep us willing to listen, learn, and perform whatever the task. In Jesus' name, amen.

Your Game Plan

Take time to reflect and jot down your thoughts using these prompts:

IN PLAY: How can you put the principle from today's devotion into practice?

PADDLE UP: Write a prayer inspired by today's Scripture or message.

Serving Up Light:
Reflecting Christ On and Off the Court

Shining God's love wherever we are

"In the same way, let your light shine before others, so that they may see your good works and give glory to your Father who is in heaven."
Matthew 5:16 (ESV)

As soon as I picked up a paddle for the first time and strode nervously onto the court, I fell in love with the game. When my long-gone carpenters promised I'd like it, their prediction was an understatement. Today, I'm actively involved with three local pickleball clubs, and the sport has become an integral part of my life: a place of connection, fun, and spiritual reflection.

Even more surprising is that six local pastors share my love for the game. We could hold a prayer meeting right on the court! It turns out faith finds a way onto the pickleball court too.

One day after a match, I walked off the court with Pastor Jeff, who leads a church that offers daily pickleball sessions. I was impressed that, while pickleball may not directly fill his pews, it broadens the perspective of God's people. Pastor Jeff's Sunday sermon challenged us to be "the light of the world" (Matthew 5:16 ESV), and this church obviously believed that pickleball could be a platform for that light.

Whether we're serving up lob shots or engaging in post-game conversations, we're called to be Christ's ambassadors. Our words and actions should reflect His love and truth, even in the most unexpected places, like a pickleball court.

When we live out our faith, we demonstrate what it means to follow Christ in real, tangible ways. Remember, we might be the only Bible someone ever reads. We need to ask ourselves if our lives shine with the love of Jesus. Do our actions inspire others to see the light of Christ like a moth to a light?

Heavenly Father, put us where we can shine for You today, whether on or off the court. May our words, deeds, thoughts, and concerns point others to You. In Jesus' name, amen.

Your Game Plan

Take time to reflect and jot down your thoughts using these prompts:

IN PLAY: How can you put the principle from today's devotion into practice?

PADDLE UP: Write a prayer inspired by today's Scripture or message.

The Perfect Partner:
Trusting God to Lead

Finding strength in partnership with Christ

"My flesh and my heart may fail, but God is the strength of my heart and my portion forever." Psalm 73:26 (ESV)

Imagine this scenario: I'm left-handed, paired with a right-handed partner, and neither talks about court coverage before the game starts. Then comes the first ball hit right down the middle. We both hesitate, glance at each other, and the ball drops untouched. *Ouch!* Moments like these remind me that even the best players can't win without good communication.

To avoid this confusion, before the game begins, I always tell my partner that I'm a "lefty." This small step compels us to discuss which of us will take the middle shots. The perfect partner works in tandem with you, not against you. We create a winning team when we understand and play to each other's strengths.

Unfortunately, not everyone welcomes a lefty on the court. Some partners assume my differences are weaknesses and either poach the ball or second-guess my abilities. Although that's disheartening, the situation has taught me something valuable: The best partners don't overshadow you; they empower you.

In our spiritual journey, Jesus is the ultimate perfect partner. He knows our strengths and weaknesses and walks with us through every challenge. Just as effective court communication enhances teamwork, open communication with Jesus strengthens our faith and guides us toward His purpose.

When I think about my faults and shortcomings, I am encouraged by Psalm 73:26: "My flesh and my heart may fail, but God is the strength of my heart and my portion forever." Jesus doesn't see our weaknesses as limitations. Instead, He uses them as opportunities to display His strength and grace in our lives.

How often do we hesitate to communicate with Jesus, much like those awkward moments on the pickleball court? Have you ever felt unsure about how to bring your struggles to Him? Remember, He is *always* available to listen, guide, and encourage us. In fact, He knows us far better than we know ourselves, so we can be sure that our requests for help will never surprise Him, nor will they ever go unanswered. We can confidently face any challenge with Him, knowing we are never alone. Hebrews 13:5 (ESV) assures us, "I will never leave you nor forsake you."

Dear Lord, thank You for being the perfect partner in our lives. Teach us to acknowledge our weaknesses, needs, fears, concerns, and joys, knowing Your grace is sufficient for us. Your hand is always outstretched, ready to walk in tandem with us. In Jesus' name, amen.

Your Game Plan

Take time to reflect and jot down your thoughts using these prompts:

IN PLAY: How can you put the principle from today's devotion into practice?

PADDLE UP: Write a prayer inspired by today's Scripture or message.

Bend Your Knees:
Practicing Prayer and Pickleball

Growing closer to God through prayer

"And they went to a place called Gethsemane. And he said to his disciples, 'Sit here while I pray.'" Mark 14:32 (ESV)

Have you ever had a catchy jingle or phrase looping in your mind, and you can't shake it? For my fellow pickleball players in the Jackson Area Pickleball Association, one chant became a hallmark of our games: "Bend your knees, Louise!"

This phrase began as a playful yet practical reminder for players who hit the ball into the net at the kitchen line—the non-volley zone. Proper technique requires bending your knees to lift the ball over the net with the appropriate arc, and this friendly chant soon became a staple. In fact, pickleball enthusiast Karen Worthy and I cowrote a children's picture book titled *Bend Your Knees, Louise! A Pickleball Primer.*

This practice of repetition and focus on technique in pickleball parallels how prayer and studying God's Word refine our relationship with Him. Just as bending our knees prepares us for success on the court, bending our knees in regular prayer, literally or figuratively, prepares our hearts for spiritual growth.

When I took a pilgrimage to Israel, I knew that the Garden of Gethsemane would be the perfect place to reflect on the significance of prayer. I sat in the actual garden where Christ prayed hours before His crucifixion, and the words of Mark 14:32 came alive: "And they went to a place called Gethsemane. And he said to his disciples, 'Sit here while I pray.'"

Jesus, the Son of God, felt the need to pray regularly. How much more do we, in our frailty, need to prioritize prayer in our lives? Seeing the power of His prayer life, His disciples asked Him to teach them to pray. His response was "The Lord's Prayer," a simple yet profound template for communication with God (Matthew 6:9–13).

We don't have to bend our knees physically for God to hear us. What matters is a sincere heart and a listening ear. Prayer isn't about rituals or perfect words but honest, heartfelt communication with our heavenly Father. Prayer is a privilege, and like practicing a good serve or mastering a technique in pickleball, it requires consistency.

If you haven't already, I invite you to make prayer a daily habit. Prayer is not a task to check off but a way to grow closer to the One who loves you most.

Dear Lord, thank You for the privilege of calling on You in prayer at any hour of the day or night. I know You love me and have plans for my life. Help me to work harder to communicate with you, prioritizing prayer. Help all Your people make prayer a habit in our lives, just as Your Son did. In Jesus' name, amen.

Your Game Plan

Take time to reflect and jot down your thoughts using these prompts:

IN PLAY: How can you put the principle from today's devotion into practice?

PADDLE UP: Write a prayer inspired by today's Scripture or message.

Pickleball, Purpose, and People: Finding Joy in the Game of Life

Connecting with others through faith and fellowship

"There is a time for everything, and a season for every activity under the heavens: [...] a time to weep and a time to laugh, a time to mourn and a time to dance." Ecclesiastes 3:1,4 (NIV)

When my husband passed away after more than forty years of marriage, I found myself in a season of profound loss. At a friend's gentle nudge, I picked up a paddle for the first time and quickly discovered that I loved the game but had much to learn. Enthusiastically, I stuck with it, and to my surprise, I discovered not just a sport but a life lesson wrapped up in a pickleball.

Ecclesiastes 3:1–4 reminds us that life flows in seasons: a time to mourn and a time to dance, a time to focus, and a time to laugh. Pickleball has become a reflection of this rhythm for me.

A Time to Focus

The game demands concentration. You must keep your eye on the ball and anticipate your opponent's moves. Similarly, life calls us to focus on what matters most, no matter the season of our lives. We are required to complete the tasks we've been given while knowing that our Father in heaven is focused on our journey, not our to-do lists.

A Time to React

Pickleball is fast paced. We don't always have time to plan our next move. We react. Life can be like that, too, unpredictable and messy.

But in life, we have the best possible partner: One who loves us completely, strengths and weaknesses. It is His strength we are to rely on throughout life.

A Time to Laugh

Let's be honest. Pickleball is fun! We've been told that laughter is the best medicine, and this game offers many occasions for laughter, even when we aren't doing well. Similarly, even in hard seasons, God's grace is present and worth celebrating. King David set us a marvelous example of the joy and laughter he shared on his walk with God, good times and bad times, both in his life and in the Psalms he left for us.

Beyond the game itself, pickleball fosters a unique sense of community. Players from all walks of life come together and form bonds. On the court, every player matters, novice or pro; in life, every individual is cherished by God, no matter their strengths or weaknesses.

Lord, thank You for the rhythms and wisdom You weave into our days. Thank You for the gift of community that a paddle, a ball, and a partner can provide, and thank You for the reminder that we all have a far greater community in Your family. In Jesus' name, amen.

Your Game Plan

Take time to reflect and jot down your thoughts using these prompts:

IN PLAY: How can you put the principle from today's devotion into practice?

PADDLE UP: Write a prayer inspired by today's Scripture or message.

Anything:
When Fear Meets Faith

Trusting God to guide us through uncertainty

"You will keep in perfect peace those whose minds are steadfast, because they trust in you. Trust in the Lord forever, for the Lord, the Lord himself, is the Rock eternal." Isaiah 26:3-4 (NIV)

Karen Worthy, my coauthor for *Bend Your Knees, Louise! A Pickleball Primer* is a close friend on and off the court. An excellent player, she organizes local pickleball tournaments and travels everywhere to play. She is a woman with resources and resilience.

One day, Karen was overseeing a local tournament. She said to me, "Jackie, you said you would do anything to help today. Can you step in and play because someone didn't show up?"

As I laced my pickleball shoes, I realized I'd promised to help with whatever she needed for the tournament. I'd thought that meant setting up tables, registering players, or handing out medals—not stepping onto the court without any warm-up while I was still recovering from recent foot surgery. But when a player didn't show, Karen turned to me, and I knew my answer had to be yes.

That moment got me thinking about another commitment I've made: my promise to God. How often have I told Him, "I'll do anything You need me to do," only to hesitate when the opportunity arose?

"Anything" sounds noble in a prayer but feels daunting in action. What if I'm not ready? What if I'm not good enough? What if someone else is better equipped?

I'm not alone in these feelings. Moses hesitated when God called him to lead, asking, "Pardon your servant, Lord. Please send someone else" (Exodus 4:13 NIV). The prophet Jeremiah, too, protested his youth and inexperience. Yet, God's response to their objections—and ours—is always the same: I will be with you.

In the heat of life's challenges, we're reminded of Paul's words in 2 Corinthians 12:9: "My grace is sufficient for you, for my power is made perfect in weakness." Long ago, I heard a wise preacher tell me, "God doesn't call the equipped; He equips the called."

That day on the pickleball court, I wasn't the best player. I didn't complain. I showed up, paddle in hand, and played my best under the circumstances. Similarly, God isn't asking for perfection. He's asking for a willing heart, ready to serve even when we feel unprepared.

What would happen if we said yes to God with the same enthusiasm we bring to the things we love, like pickleball? Let's be people who mean it when we say, "Lord, I'll do anything."

Heavenly Father, thank You for calling us into Your service, even when we feel unprepared. Give us the courage to say yes no matter the task, and equip us with Your grace and wisdom to follow through with a joyful heart. In Jesus' name, amen.

Your Game Plan

Take time to reflect and jot down your thoughts using these prompts:

IN PLAY: How can you put the principle from today's devotion into practice?

PADDLE UP: Write a prayer inspired by today's Scripture or message.

Good Game:
Celebrating with Grace

Finishing well and giving glory to God

"Do everything without grumbling or arguing, so that you may become blameless and pure, 'children of God without fault in a warped and crooked generation.' Then you will shine among them like stars in the sky." Philippians 2:14–15 (NIV)

"Good game."

In pickleball, after the final point is made, players meet at the net to tap paddles and say, "Good game." This small but meaningful tradition of sportsmanship acknowledges effort and camaraderie, regardless of the outcome. But let's be honest: Sometimes, "good game" isn't spoken with the best attitude.

Have you ever found yourself grumbling after a loss? Complaining about the shots your partner missed or the calls your opponent made? I sure have. Frustration can easily steal the joy right out of the game.

Life can feel like a competition, and when someone else "wins," I'm tempted to grumble about how unfair it feels or how much better things should have gone for me. But Scripture is clear: We're called to "do everything without complaining or arguing" (Philippians 2:14). That includes the moments when life doesn't go our way.

So, how do we shift our focus? Philippians 4:8–9 (MSG) gives us a beautiful perspective: "You'll do best by filling your minds and meditating on things true, noble, reputable, authentic, compelling, gracious—the best, not the worst; the beautiful, not the ugly; things to praise, not things to curse."

Instead of dwelling on mistakes or unfairness, we can choose to celebrate the effort, opportunity, and lessons learned. Imagine how much brighter we'd shine as followers of Christ if we met life's outcomes—both wins and losses—with gratitude and grace. Whether it's a pickleball match or a challenging season, we're called to reflect God's love and joy, pointing others to Him through our attitude.

Next time you meet someone at life's "net," try tapping paddles with genuine humility, whether celebrating a victory or learning from a loss. It's not just good sportsmanship; it's a testimony to Christ's work in your life.

Lord, help us forego grumbling and complaining so we can focus instead on what is true, noble, and beautiful. Teach us to reflect Your love in all circumstances so others may see You in our actions and attitudes. May we always strive to shine Your light for Your glory, not our own. In Jesus' name, amen.

Your Game Plan

Take time to reflect and jot down your thoughts using these prompts:

IN PLAY: How can you put the principle from today's devotion into practice?

PADDLE UP: Write a prayer inspired by today's Scripture or message.

FINAL REFLECTION

Final Reflection

Carrying the Game and the Gospel

In 2020, the world paused, and so did sports. The NBA found itself in an unprecedented situation, playing in a tightly controlled bubble at Walt Disney World's ESPN Wide World of Sports Complex. With no fans and limited interaction, downtime became a challenge for everyone involved: players, coaches, and referees.

Enter Scott Foster, a veteran NBA referee, who brought something unexpected into the bubble: a pickleball net. What started as a way for referees to pass the time caught the attention of the basketball players. Soon, some of the NBA's biggest stars were stepping onto the pickleball court, learning the basics, and experiencing the fun of the game.

Watching this unfold offered a moment of clarity for me. Here were elite athletes, masters of basketball, captivated by the simplicity and joy of pickleball. They gave me and others a glimpse into the future of the sport. Foster's decision to bring pickleball into the bubble may have seemed small, but it ignited a spark that helped propel the sport into the mainstream.

That spark reminds me of how we're called to carry our faith wherever we go. Just as Foster introduced pickleball to the basketball world, we have the opportunity to introduce the light of Christ into every space we enter. Whether through our words, actions, or attitudes, we can influence those around us, sometimes in ways we may never fully realize.

The lesson here is simple but profound: Never underestimate the power of showing up with what you have. Foster didn't come to the NBA bubble intending to change the trajectory of a sport; he just brought what he loved into a new space. Similarly, we don't have to orchestrate grand gestures to make an impact. If we live out our faith authentically and intentionally, we can trust God to use our efforts for His purposes.

As this book concludes, I invite you to consider where you can bring your faith and passion. What court has God placed you on? How can you let His light shine through you in ways that might inspire others?

Like pickleball, faith brings people together, sparks joy, and transforms lives. May we each leave this "court" ready to carry the game—and the gospel—into the world. You never know whose life you might change.

About the Author

Jackie Freeman is a storyteller at heart, whether through the written word, speaking engagements, or everyday conversations. As a writer and speaker, she encourages others to find joy along the journey, no matter the season of life.

Jackie lives on a sixty-acre farm in Michigan, where she and her late husband raised three sons and made lasting memories. Today, you might find her tending her garden and pulling weeds (both literal and spiritual), while listening for God's voice. When she's not on the farm, you might find her on a pickleball court, sharing the game she loves or preparing for the next adventure God is calling her to.

Her passion is to inspire others to see God's hand at work—in life's victories, losses, and every moment in between. She encourages others to stand firmly in God's Word and embrace His will, whether in times of abundance or seasons of waiting.

Please connect with Jackie Freeman at:
www.jackiefreemanauthor.com.

If you enjoyed *Pickleball Parables: Inspiration On and Off the Court*, please consider reviewing it on Amazon, so more people can discover it.

To book Jackie as a speaker for your next event, visit www.jackiefreemanauthor.com/speaker.

Bend Your Knees, Louise!: A Pickleball Primer

This best-selling children's picture book introduces young readers to the sport of pickleball through engaging rhyme and vibrant illustrations. Perfect for families, teachers, and coaches, it makes learning the game fun.

Unwrapping Christmas: Advent 4 Week Devotional

An Advent devotional that invites readers to rediscover the meaning of Christmas through the lens of twelve beloved carols. Each reflection connects timeless lyrics with Scripture and personal application, and is accompanied by a Spotify playlist that enhances the devotional experience throughout the season.

Keep a Song in Your Heart: Musical Notes for Daily Devotions

This devotional seamlessly blends faith and music, drawing inspiration from beloved hymns and timeless spiritual songs. Each devotion reflects on a meaningful lyric and offers encouragement, Scripture, and a specially curated Spotify playlist to deepen the reader's connection to God through music.

Journal for a JOYful Heart

songs of spring
songs of summer
songs of autumn
songs of winter

Designed to encourage reflection and gratitude in every season of life, this guided journal series offers Scripture, thoughtful prompts, and a Spotify playlist to inspire personal growth. Whether embracing new beginnings, savoring moments of joy, or finding peace in life's transitions, each journal provides a space to draw closer to God.

I'm Okay, Momma!

A heartwarming picture book that illustrates the fruit of the Spirit through the daily interactions of a mother and child. With gentle rhymes and relatable moments, it helps children recognize how love, kindness, and patience manifest in their world, while offering parents opportunities to demonstrate these traits.

Strength in the Storm (Beatitudes Publishing)
God with Us Immanuel (Redemption Press)

Jackie Freeman is a contributing author in *Strength in the Storm* (Beatitudes Publishing), a powerful collection of true stories from women who found unwavering faith in the midst of life's fiercest battles.

She also shares her heart in *God with Us Immanuel* (Redemption Press), an inspiring anthology that celebrates the hope and presence of Christ in every season.

Through these works, Jackie offers encouragement and truth to readers seeking God's light in dark places.